Define Me
Divine Me

D0923826

A Poetic Display of Affection
by Phoebe Garnsworthy

Also By Phoebe Garnsworthy:
Lost Nowhere: A Journey of Self-Discovery (Vol. 1)
Lost Now Here: The Road to Healing (Vol. 2)
Daily Rituals: Positive Affirmations to Attract Love,
Happiness, and Peace
The Spirit Guides: A Short Novella

Define Me / Divine Me : A Poetic Display of Affection - 1st ed.
ISBN: 978-0-9954119-20
Paperback
Copyright © 2019 by **Phoebe Garnsworthy**
Artwork by Evelyn Lorenz

www.PhoebeGarnsworthy.com

Can you feel it?

There's a shift in consciousness.

We are learning a new way to love ourselves,

and it's working.

dedication to you

Just a little note to say thank you.
Thank you for showing the strength within me
when I thought I had none. Thank you for seeing the
beauty inside me when I felt anything less than
worthy. Thank you for pushing me forward, when all
I wanted to do was turn back around. It's the little
words of encouragement that help me be a better me,
that help me fight through the day, and I'm so
grateful to have you in my life.

Contents

introduction

Define Me Divine Me: A Poetic Display of Affection is an exploration of raw truth that provokes our deepest emotions so that we may honor both the light and the dark within us all. Together, we allow the words of enlightened wisdom and painful beginnings to wash through us, as we stand back up and claim what is rightfully ours. As you devour these words with precision, you too will reflect on your own life's journey, and realize that we are more connected than once thought. The idealism of loneliness will expire, and a new celebration of unity will take its place.

Our journey inwards is never-ending, and the wisdom we are learning, we already know. It's just a matter of removing the layers of our perceived reality and embedded beliefs to get to the core of our Eternal Self. So that we may reveal who it is that we really are: A Divine Creation of Angelic Energy.

And as you choose to show the world your authentic self, you will find the peace, happiness, and love that you are seeking. Here is your new vocabulary to raise your vibration higher, or to sit with the shadows if that is what you seek. It is a creative space to nurture and inspire your restless Soul. An eclectic mix of vibrations molded into words from me to you.

from the author

I loved sharing these fractions of my Soul with you.
When I write, I connect to a Source bigger than me,
and greater than my own understanding. It's an
entity too vast to be defined, and too incredibly
powerful to be explained. But when I sit and write,
I lose all control over the power of my pen to paper
as I tap into the abundance of infinity, what I believe
to be the collective unconscious. And as I dance
through these streams of vibrations, I channel them
into something tangible: words to define a moment,
an emotion, an experience of our lives.

Define Me Divine Me: A Poetic Display of Affection is a
personal collection of poetry and prose, woven with
spiritual wisdom and shadows of the ego.

When writing this book I entered a space buried deep
within myself that I had locked up tight. Slithers of
light seeped through at times yet the darkness caged
its fate. This wounded feeling of loneliness overtook
any ideas of hope that connection existed, and at
times I preferred to close my eyes to the truth. But a
life living in fear, scared of our weaknesses and
shamed of our scars, was no way to live.

So as I became more comfortable with the depth of beauty and profound mystery within me, it was a natural progression to let the light shine through and triumph over the dark, filling my heart with love. Only this time with more gratitude, for now the light feels warmer and brighter than it ever did before.

Everything that is hinted at aims to draw emotion from the reader to remind them of their own journey. Their own troubles and mishaps. It is designed to help weed through our mind and life to see the light. Through a poetic display of affection, we will together honor our emotions and remember our connection and unity as one.

Love Phoebe xo

Define Me
Divine Me

A Poetic Display of Affection
by Phoebe Garnsworthy

you are worthy

You deserve a life full of great things
overflowing with happiness, magic, and love.
But to get there, you need to believe in it too.
Believe in yourself
and believe that there is good in the world.
And when you finally do, it will come to you.
And when this day comes you will realize
that it's been there all along.
You've just decided to open your eyes to see it for
what it was…

in the beginning

Today I had a moment of clarity.
A glimpse of the truth,
the answer to my prayers.
It is that I am powerful beyond comprehension,
that I am creating every second of my world.
All the heartbreak, the pain—is my doing.
For it's the only way I can evolve into the person that
I need to become.
It's all happening for a reason.
And that reason is to awaken
the Divine Light within me.

But I've realized
that I cannot go on living as I used to,
for my Soul is yearning for a change in my life.
Commanding that I do something different.
Asking to use the gifts that I am given.
And I have no other choice but to listen.
For the voices will continue to scream
loud within my heart.
From today on I vow that I will do as it pleases.
Allow me to flow with the Universe, reveal the depth
of my creativity, inspiration, and love.
It's the only way for me to be free.
It's the only way to live a happy life,
and the happiness of my life is entirely up to me.

pathway to freedom

Blossoming into our true self
takes time and patience.
First, we must tend to
the inner cravings of our Soul,
and listen with confidence
to the callings of our heart.
Then, we nurture and praise
what it is that makes us truly happy.
And once all this is done,
then we will stand strong within our own light.

the real me

I yearn to awaken the real me,
the bold me,
the unapologetic raw me.
The nice me, the kind me,
the unconditional loving me,
the truthful, honest and true me.
She's somewhere deep inside of me
forced to hide, forced to cover
because of the ashamed me,
the insecure me,
the hard-to-please me,
the stubborn and regretful me...
But I will BE no longer.
Because the hopeful me,
the evolving me,
the resilient me,
the goddess in me
knows the truth.
And it's only a matter of time
before the real me,
the divine me,
the gracious, kind and wild me
is set free...

i am enough

Everything you need is already within you.
— that sense of security,
— that feeling of acceptance,
— that desire to understand the purpose of your life
and to live in harmonious bliss.
It's all there, ready to be recognized.
For you have all the answers you need right now.
All you need to do is close your eyes and listen.

universal kin

You are a child of the Universe,
A creator of true love.
There is a light in your heart
that grows more powerful every day.
And even the darkness that you hold
just helps the beauty inside you glow brighter
with brilliance,
with radiance,
and courage.
So do not fear.
You are supported always.
Open your heart and receive
the blessings of the Divine.

upside down

In one moment it all changed.
Everything that once was, wasn't anymore.
It had nowhere to go, but to be gone (disappear).
All the old beliefs were discarded from her being,
and she had no other choice but to adopt new ideas.
How terribly frightening
and wonderfully freeing at the same time!
To awaken to a world that she thought she had
figured out, yet turned out she did not know at all.
Her quest for understanding had just begun.
As a curious mind overtook all fear and rationality.
She was flowing with the sea breeze,
flying in the clouds,
allowing the Universe to push and pull
and twist her upside down.

the need for change

And just like that, she disappeared.
Her voice was drained from screaming
empty words that held substance to her,
but not to them.
It didn't matter too much.
The noise didn't really exist, it was all in her head.
But that was just it — it was her reality.
And it was her choice to jump in and out
and move as she liked.
It was time for a change.
The seas were calling her.
She needed to go.
Seek new landscapes and distant horizons.
A muddy patch of salt water
contrasting the dimly lit sky.
It was a change, and to her it was beautiful.
For it encompassed everything
she ever wanted and more.
The unusual portrayal of beauty,
of dark matter amongst a starry night sky.

searching

I don't feel like I belong here.
My days are filled with empty faces
and loveless souls.
And time wasted on things that don't matter.
I think about what it would be like to leave this
world, but... I know that I can't give up that easily.
For, I still believe that there is someone out there to
connect with.
Someone who thinks and feels
the same way that I do.
Someone who loves without fear,
and speaks from the depth of their heart.
Who spends their days admiring
the beauty still left in this world.
And when I find that person I will know
and we will share our time with real experiences,
remind each other of the truth of our existence.
And create a temple full of sweet vibrations
and healing tones
in a love nest far, far away.
I can feel their energy is near and coming,
and I manifest with loving light
on the energy from the moon,
that we will find each other one day
in this broken world
full of forgotten dreams
and heartless souls.

misled

Mixed feelings of confusion,
of searching for familiarity.
Knowing that this is the choice
that I have made every day and yet the meaning
behind it is lost in translation.
My heart yearns for the beach,
for my golden lands of home,
for the sound of birds and animals—
A glimmer of life around me.
It's easy to feel dead in a city that's always sleeping.
In a city that moves as slowly as a calm stream.
And I am floating down it.
But I hold onto the rocks on the side,
terrified to keep going.
Knowing that I hate to swim in the cold.
I want to reside on the land,
beneath the sun, safe on the ground.
Little did I know…
That the fishes were swimming alongside me.
Little did I know there was a whole world of wonder
just waiting to be found.
And it was sitting silently
just waiting for me
to let go,
to move on,
and open my eyes.

other side

She often dreamed about another land,
another life, another time.
But when it finally came
nothing was as she expected.
The journey, the world, the life.
She needed new eyes,
a new perspective.
a different beginning
for the same story.
For it was as she always was.
The growth of waves,
chopping and churning with no pattern.
Same life, but a different world.

starvation

And I walk past people but do they see me?
Really, truly see me.
I feel like I am a floating face,
an empty space of energy.
That longs for connection,
and yet feels comfort in solitude.
I feel more alive
in the silent spaces between our words.
And I long for my time alone,
more so than with another person.
It's a moment when I can breathe and just be me.
The tender, naked, and satisfied me.

touch

My Soul is starving for real connections...
Talk to me about your passions,
your desire to be a better you,
your acts of self-love and self-care.
How do you feed your Soul's desires?
Let's share the wisdom of our ancestors
and contemplate the energies of the Universe,
as we pick flowers
and drink plant medicines
and dance around the fire,
and celebrate life, love,
and all the magnificent mysteries in the world.

remember

I've forgotten what it's like to be myself again.
And I'm standing in the ocean drowning alone.
Waiting for the days to feel alive again,
waiting for the sun to shine upon me once more.
I know the answers
that I need to move through this:
Embrace the depths of my emotion
in the same honor as I do my light.
For if this feeling is to pass
I must acknowledge and release it.
Remember that it's merely a wave washing over me.
And soon I will be dry
standing in my warmth,
in my light, and in my truth.
It's just a phase.
It's just a phase.
It's just a phase I'm going through.
Tomorrow will be better.
Tomorrow is another day.

timelapse

The thick black coal of darkness,
of death,
of the corrupt nature of one's mind
transferring to another.
The bleeding cries of hope and despair.
Wanting so badly to mean something in this world,
unaware that you already do.

the way forward

Fire: Burn the lies you are telling yourself,
and reveal the truth inside your heart.

Earth: Open your wounds and let the ground heal
you, filling you up with nurturing love.

Air: Breathe deeply to seek clarity on your life,
you will realize you are being guided according to
the Divine time.

Water: Cleanse, refresh, and allow yourself to rebirth
into a new and improved version of who it is that
you wish to become.

new moon

There are invisible plans waiting to be hatched.
And as I enter this beautiful space,
I ask to be true to myself
and stand strong in my own light.
I wish for peace, happiness, and health
to all around me.
I pray for true love to enter my life,
and if now is not the right time,
then please gift me the grace and patience to accept
what is, and not force something that is not.
Angels, please stay by my side.
I can feel the breakthrough of transformation is near.

rivers

There is a river of stillness within me.
A flow of energy that basks in light,
that echoes peace and harmony through its currents.
And yet sometimes I forget how to swim.
I drown within my own lightness of being,
and I refuse to accept
that I hold such love within me.
And so I go,
from stream to stream,
river to river,
searching to swim with another.
All the while forgetting
that I have a river of stillness within me.

patience

Sometimes we are faced with conflict.
An uphill battle
as though the race has already been won.
But it's times like these when miracles happen.
When the impossible becomes possible.
Because you are always supported by Grace.

familiar

You remind me of what it's like to feel in love again.
With my naked flesh submerged
in the warmth of your skin,
my body molds into your creases perfectly
like a puzzle.
And your drumming heartbeat echoes
faintly in my ears as I lie on your chest
and take deep breaths in sync with yours.
Your natural smell calms me
like I am one with my family.
And I close my eyes in peace,
knowing there is no harm to be felt.
I can drift off to sleep, to dance in my dreams,
knowing I will have safety when I open my eyes.

different

He was madness that was sure, but she knew it.
It was exactly what she needed;
a gothic backdrop to frame the light she held inside.

attachment

As she listened with her heart,
she closed her vulnerability up.
It's what attracted them to her.
She was unable to be understood,
unable to be transparent.
It was her greatest strength
and weakness at the same time.
Only he was able to break through to her,
and that is why she couldn't let him go.

wild

If only honesty won the hearts of strangers.
Instead, we must hide our weirdness
in the hopes that they will like us.
And so we build a cage around our Soul,
allowing us to fly "free"
inside our own chosen parameters.

But imagine…
If you dared to reveal the truth
of who you really are.
And if you found someone who not only loved you,
but encouraged you to be the wildest version of
yourself that you could be.
Imagine how you would feel
living a life lived like that.

boundaries

Those things they said that are your weaknesses
are actually your strengths.
The world needs more sensitivity,
more selfless lovers, more generosity,
more givers.
Just learn your own limits
of when the giving becomes too much.
Boundaries exist for a reason.

against

It's a constant battle against my internal thoughts.
Of being true to myself,
and the person I wish to become.
I am trying so hard to please him,
but I feel as though it is not enough.
Oh, how I look forward to the combat being over.
To feel settled at home and in peace on my own.
Every morning is a new day,
and he is innocent in my arms.
Everything from the day before has been forgotten
and a new version of our life together begins.
But some days are harder than others.
And the fear creeps in.
Fear that we cannot make our dream a reality.
Scared that our love song
has played too many times before.
And so I pretend.
I smile with my crying eyes.
Carefully watching, knowing and understanding,
that this idealism of perfection is slipping through
my hands.

foolish

I can foresee the danger, and I'm falling down.
But it's too late, I've already lost balance.
Where once I would've flown aimlessly with
confidence, now I cower thinking my love is doomed.
But at the end of the day, are we all just fools? Falling
hopelessly in love with the wrong kind of people.

confrontation

They were lucky to have had someone like you in their life. Someone who gave love so freely, who shared positivity with ease. You weren't being too much yourself, you were perfectly right. It's just that they weren't right for you. You didn't do anything wrong. You were simply speaking your truth. Because when your true love comes along they will praise that spark inside your Soul, applaud that energy within your mind, and breathe even more life toward the fire that blazes from your heart.

hands

And for every second that goes by
without you.
I lie hopelessly
holding my own hand
and telling myself
everything is going to be all right.

crazy

"Release me from this madness," I pray.
And I scream
as thunderous voices echo inside my head.
"You are the only one who can save you," it says.

shooting star

The star flew by quickly in the night sky.
It burst into flames and she made a wish.
But it wasn't as simple as the idea was to her.
She wanted something more…
To escape her life.
So often she wished that she could do the same,
blaze for a second and then disappear.

love

Love,
such a surreal experience.
Emotion. Devotion.
No questioning it. It just is.
And yet,
despite the strength of how full my love is for you
if my boundaries are broken it will be no more.
There is no hate in its place,
For then, I would suffer too.
Instead, I would still love you.
I just would not be "in love" with you.
And the difference is that I can sleep at night,
knowing that I love me more.

fencing

The stronger fighter is the one who walks away from battle before it has even begun.

pray

I call upon the Heavens from above.
May you protect me as I sleep peacefully.
And when I awake tomorrow,
may I be open to whatever crosses my path.
I know you are always guiding me
toward my greatest good
(even if I don't understand it).
Bless me with confidence and clarity
to go about my day,
and help me transit smoothly
into what it is that I must achieve.

moving through

You need to just let it go.
You've been waiting for too long
and nothing has changed.
Now it's time to live your life
and let them live theirs.
Have comfort in knowing that there's love between
you two and if you are meant to be together it will
happen one day, when the alignment is right.

fighter

So, what now?
Now you live.
Now you take back your power and forgive them.
But their actions do not go unnoticed.
They have tried to break your spirit,
tried to shake you up,
and kill the love that you have for yourself.
They have tried to ruin you.
But they don't know what you are capable of.
They don't know how strong you are.
How much love you have for yourself.
They thought you were weak.
Well now is your time to show them
they were wrong.

release

I take back all the power I gave away.
And likewise, release all energy that is not mine.
For I cannot be who I truly am with all this
toxicity weighing me down.
Let go of me, and I will of you.
So that we can be full on our own.
And let the Divine Light from within our heart
spread joy to the world alone.

no more

Every now and again, the memory still haunts me.
It robs me of the present moment,
forcing me to stumble backward.

Why must I punish myself any longer?
Why do I keep the thoughts of misery still alive?

Today, no longer.
Today, I forgive myself.
Today, I let go and move on.

forward

Every step is bringing me closer to my destiny.
My vibration is raised.
I am listening to my heart.
I am speaking the truth from my Soul.
Spirit is here to guide me.
I close my eyes and feel the way to my truth.

the internal struggle

she cries in the shadows
where she thinks no one can see her.
but her guides up above are looking down,
wishing she would listen.
She's unaware that these encounters
are what's building her character.
Putting a sword in her hand
and an armor on her chest to protect her,
she feels heavy.
But soon it will mold into her body and fit
like a thick layer of skin,
and the next time around
she will move quicker than before.
More graceful, more subtle.
More lighter than ever.
She will slither into battle.
and laugh at her triumph
but not just for the winning.
For she now knows that the pain was to be endured
so that success could be defined.

letters to myself

I despise the notion of regret and yet somehow I am
in an agreement that my life has become sadly thus.
And although I hold strength in the idealism that
everything happens for a reason,
my happiness is hard to define.
Repeatedly for years, I have aligned myself with
positivity yet slowly over time such passion fades.
Like the white in our eyes once clear with youth,
it withers over time.
Burnt by the sun,
and stung by the sea,
they mourn too.
I want to create my own security.
Be my own role model,
my own light, laughter, and love.
I want. I want. I want.
When I already am enough.
I've just forgotten.
I've forgotten how to pat my own back.
Smile to myself in the mirror
and sing with joy in the shower.
Because the water dries up too quickly,
and I stand here staring for hours.
Remembering how good it once was
to feel alive.

what i need

I'm not delicate.
I don't pretend to be.
I'm both strong and vulnerable, raw yet protected,
Truthful, honest, and open.
I need a lover who shares my intensity.
Who meets me in the center of my heart
and reveals themselves too.
With passion and commitment
we will unite together.
Seeing past the exterior
we will bare each other's Souls.
Ravishing the depth of our core,
and praising the light in our eyes.
Feeling, touching, breathing, and living.
Rejoicing and illuminating the love between us.
As we hold each other we will whisper great love
stories, and imprint them in the stars,
to claim them next lifetime.
And to hear the echoes of I love you,
for an eternity more.

adorn

I was searching for love
in places where love didn't exist.
Trying to seal validation
for self-worth and self-acceptance.
Aching to be told that I was pretty,
beautiful or intelligent.
Unaware that I was the one
who created those definitions myself.
I foolishly thought it was okay
to give another that kind of power.
I stupidly believed I needed approval from everyone
else, but myself.
So when I finally stopped looking outside
and searched within I found the answer
to all of my problems.
And I rejoiced with victory
thinking my confusions would all be over.

But the journey of self-love was just beginning
and never-ending.
It's a continuous cycle
of remembering such simple truths:

—I am love,
—I am worthy of love,
—I am all that I am.

It's an endless battle
to keep the love inside of me alight.
And, so I remind myself with love notes and flowers
and things that make me smile.
Decorating my sacred space with crystals,
and candles, and sweet-smelling perfumes.
Creating my own existence externally to mirror the
love and affection that I hold inside.

letters to myself, part 2

Every day I am challenged with my own mind.
I thought I had forgotten this taste and yet it had
always somewhere stained my mouth. My simple
daily routine feels far from achievable and yet there is
no reason for such misery to exist. Perhaps it's the
result of being surrounded by toxic energies around
me. When I am near them, I can only feel my mind
screaming to run away. And I hate being that girl.
I hate feeling this way, I hate the word hate...
Trying so hard to overcome these feelings of
emotions, the illusion of compression as if there is no
way out. I let them get the better of me. I stand in the
shallow waters and allow the waves to crash over
me, suck me under, and drown me whole. Even
though I am tall enough to walk away. When will life
become easy again?

sleeping

It's a strange feeling of emptiness
When I choose to believe the lies:
That, without him I would disappear.
That, only their love could fill me up.
But when I move through the pain
I realize
I'm here to face myself.
The depth inside of me.
Confront my demons.
I am here trying hard
and yet I don't feel like I am trying at all.
I let the emotions wash over me
but perhaps I stand too long in the water,
When I need to get out and dry myself
And start again.

balancing act

Sometimes we close our minds to heartache.
Forget the bad and only remember the good.
We dismiss the truth
that the scales tipped in the wrong direction.
It's just a lie.
A lie that we like to tell ourselves.

slipping

It's a half-moon, someone is smiling.
Exhale slowly, the smoke flows through.
I always found myself sleeping,
and then I met you.
You appeared as quickly as you left.
Your shadow piercing,
more than I could have imagined.
You tell me you just want to be.
And I forever remember you in my dreams.

combat

Today I gift myself patience and peace.
Allowing the love from my family
and ancestors to comfort my Soul.
I wish to take only the good thoughts
and positive intentions.
But, although they may not realize it,
their fears are passed on too.
But it's okay.
For I am stronger than they once were,
I have more courage,
more strength, more determination to face the day.
I combat their limiting beliefs, with a smile.
Knowing that their words cannot hurt me.
And they will never be passed on as my own.
I vow to stop the trauma from the past lives living
as I create this new world for me and my family.

move

How do you keep going
when you are in doubt of yourself?
How do you let go and start over?
It's that self-love and self-healing
you need for yourself.
A desire to be kinder to yourself,
and to practice listening to that voice in your heart
that is telling you to move on.
One step forward.
One more step forward.
Take a deep breath and try again.

savior

Are you looking for a hand to hold?
Well...
Look down.
You have two, don't you?
Put them together,
bring them close to your heart,
and now close your eyes.
Can you feel that beautiful soul inside of you?
Take a deep breath, and start again.
Everything is going to be okay.

teacher

They were never meant to stay in your life.
They just appeared to teach you a lesson.
To remind you not to lose yourself,
to tell you the relationship should always be equal.
The pain you feel will pass, my love,
and one day you will be grateful.
For it has taught you lessons you will never forget—
how to love yourself,
how to forgive yourself,
and how to heal yourself.

loneliness

Sometimes when I'm feeling lonely
I walk into book stores and breathe in their smell.
Stale pages filled with broken hearts and painful
pasts, of forgotten dreams and wasted love stories.
And suddenly, I don't feel so alone anymore.

limitless

Close your eyes and come in
to your Heart Center.
This is where you will draw your strength,
here is where you will see your Divine Light.
And when you are lonely,
all it takes is a moment of breath
and the stillness of mind to remind you of the truth—
That you are and always have been:
a Divine Creation of the Universe.

effortless

I am connected to the Divine.
My heart beats in alignment with the Universe.
And together we weave my life's journey,
an evolution of change
to become the best version of myself.
And it's only when I forget this simple truth,
that I find myself in misery and pain.
So instead, I choose to believe I am guided,
loved, and supported.
I allow myself to breathe hope that my world is
exactly everything it is meant to be and more.
There is no other way, there is no other option.
It simply is.

tossing and turning

She rode her emotions like waves in the ocean.
But too often they subsided.
Sucked her under and drowned her whole.
How did she manage to make her way out?
She learned to swim,
she learned to float,
she learned to dream
and to believe she was stronger
than she thought she ever could be.
And she realized the truth.
She could survive everything and anything—
because she was the one who created it.

perfection

Break down all those fears inside your mind
that tell you that you aren't good enough.
That makes you think that you aren't smart enough,
or pretty enough.
You are perfect exactly as you are
right at this moment.
You have so much love in your heart,
and that fulfills every definition of perfection
that there ever was.
From this love set your own definitions,
your own standard of who it is that you want to be,
and right now—
you are absolutely perfect.

climbing

The rain pours down upon me,
and I feel as though it is piercing my heart,
breaking it open and cleansing my Soul.
And I stand here naked, enamored in her beauty.
Feeling the gratitude of clarity on my skin.
The tears are watering my heart
and helping me grow through this pain.
I hate you and love you at the same time.

try again

This heartbreak is not for nothing,
no one can say that you didn't try.
You showed them how deeply your heart could open,
and how much love you held inside.
Now take all that love you gave them
(the love they weren't able to return),
And pour it over every area of yourself
and your life,
for self-love is the lesson to be learned.

yes

I know it feels like the end of the world right now.
And the easy option would be to give up
and run away.
But trust me, just don't.
Wait it out a little bit.
Something beautiful is coming to you, I promise.
It's a gift that can never be taken away.
And you're about to wake up all over again.
Unlearn what you thought you knew,
and relearn the wisdom you know
but have forgotten.
And you're going to love yourself deeper than you
could have ever thought possible.
This pain you feel will never come to you again.
The gift is here and ready for you.
Will you accept it?

breathe out

Fear of the unknown, it's only an idea.
Don't let it shake you.
Don't let the idea swallow your confidence.
It's a false idea, a limiting belief.
And you know the truth.
So face it head on, and cut it down to shreds.
You are better than that.
You are everything.
Confident, courageous and resilient.
Everything will turn out just fine.
Just you wait.

within

I close my eyes and see you.
I know that you are always with me,
but sometimes I forget.
But then you remind me.
Through the comfort of your presence,
the light inside of me is ignited.
And when I hear your voice,
I see the beauty within me
that I thought had disappeared.
As I touch my heart
you bring me back into the present moment,
and when I tell you that I love you,
I feel as I always was, the Blessed Creation
that I always have been, always will be.

pity

Sometimes all you can do is feel sorry for yourself.
It's easier that way.
And the desire to curl into a ball and disappear can
be triggered from nothing at all.
Or is it everything at once?
Somehow you find yourself living
a life you feel disconnected with.
And yet it is impossible to do anything else but
to recreate the gift of holding you
and loving you on my own.
The softest skin to touch.
Your heartbeat.
It's my favorite time of day,
just you and me and the night sky.

choices

She stands in the middle of the street,
the lights around her buzzing.
The energy is electrifying.
She doesn't know where to go.
The doors around her feel empty,
and the houses that have people in them
are calling her name.
But she doesn't want to go there.

misery

Holding onto
the past weighs heavy
on my body, heavy on my skin
and heavy on my chest.
It demolishes
any chance of hope
in my eyes.
While it rips against my flesh
peeling layers off
one by one,
as it grinds against the sand
until I am raw,
until I cry, and I do cry.
I cry with the hope of a no tomorrow.

the answer

Allow the depth of the sky to weigh down on your heart. Crushing your lungs making it impossible to breathe, so all you can do is just focus on your breath. That's the secret to anything in life, the solution to everything, just allow your breath to inhale, and exhale, listen, watch and repeat.

let it go

She lay on the ground in the dirt beneath the sun.
Feeling the burn of the rays on her chest.
The ants beneath her crawled all over her body
and in tiny bites, they stung the edges of her skin.
She liked it.
It mirrored the pain in her mind that she felt.
It soothed the fears and thoughts
that she had been believing.
And just as the pain stopped
she remembered the same.
It was only a thought, soon to pass.
Let it go.
Let it go.

like a flower

Where am I going?
There is nothing left for me here.
There is no one who understands.
I am leaving you.
You are leaving me.
Where am I going?
Back and forth between it all.
Where to go.
Where to look.
Where to breathe.
It doesn't stop,
you keep sliding through life.
Holding tight, to what?
To you?
To the sun
and the moon
and to the heavens above.
Forever this.
Forever now.
Together.
She blossoms.

evolve

Your whole world is being turned upside down
for a reason… It's because you're being asked
to awaken to a new way of life.
For a new version of you is emerging,
and when it does,
you will feel more yourself than you ever have
before. More aligned with the path of your true
destiny,
as you finally begin to live the life you have always
wished that you would.

So, go gently as you get accustomed to your new
surroundings, and be patient because everything you
have ever wanted is coming to you.
And there is no going back now to the old you.
For now, you are going to be wiser and stronger
than before.
You are going to love more deeply,
give more freely, and live with more grace.
This is the real life that you deserve.
Give up any thought that doesn't support it.
You need to open your eyes to see it.
And open your heart to believe it.

holding space

And I am holding space for you.
Right here. Right now.
With open arms and an open heart,
I will wait for you so you can be who you truly are.
And I will listen to your story so you can release
and let it rest.
And you can heal the internal wounds you breathe,
in the comfort of this space.
I will send you love and light until you reconnect
with your inner guide,
for it is somewhere deep within you,
masked beneath the shadow of your smile.

caged butterfly

I'm ready to take the risk,
and leap wild into the unknown.
And even if I end up nowhere
at least I will have spent a year of my life trying
something new that's made me feel more alive than
spending an eternity safe within the walls I've built
around myself.

easy

In an instant, everything had simplified.
What was once complex and frustrating
now felt insignificant and clear.
This was the answer.
That was the choice.
This is the way forward.
Why couldn't it always be this way? she thought.
"It is," her intuition answered,
"You just keep forgetting."

habits

Now is a time for healing.
Today, if you will allow.
Let the medicine from Spirit in
and transform your world around.
It's time to change every element of your life,
every relationship, every habit.
Nurture or remove them.
Is it supporting your Soul?
Is that energy good for you?
What do you want?
What do you need?

trust

I close my eyes and feel the beauty
of my Soul beating.
It's the anchor of truth within my heart.
The lightness of my being.
She is breathing within me
And when I'm sad, she is sad too.
But then she brews strength in my misery.
And she calls upon Grace
as I stand there in my darkness.
And she reminds me
of how perfectly timed my life is.
How everything is working in my favor.
All I need to do is believe,
and breathe,
and heal,
and trust.

change

The past can hurt you no longer.
You have learned from it,
and now it's time to let it go.
Today is a new day,
enter it with an open heart full of love
and gratitude.

rise again

And she dove deep below the ocean.
So far down,
they didn't know if she was going to resurface.
But she always did.
She knew that the salt water would cleanse her.
Make her stronger than she had ever been before.
It was a fresh start.
A new beginning.
It was the only way she knew how to survive.
And so she rose again.

earth

Today I just left everyone
and sat by myself
on the Earth
in the dirt
amongst the rocks
in nature.
With ancient tree trunks, and weeds
and flowers and
a million flora and fauna
everywhere.
The wind blew gracefully
as I fell into Mother Nature's arms.
And in this safe space she blessed me with her love,
healed me with her vibrations
and grounded my Soul into my body.
From just her touch I feel completely new again,
restored with harmony,
eager to walk with confidence and clarity
beneath the rising sun.

advisor

I asked the Universe for answers.
I said I was tired of feeling confused,
hurt, and abandoned.
She said I was my own worst enemy
and also my greatest savior.
And that I had the power to choose
which one I wanted to be.
The decision was easy.

answers

I said I needed change.
"So change," they said
I said I needed love.
"So give love to yourself," they said
I said I needed hope.
"So start believing," they said.
"It's all up to you.
You are creating your world,
and whatever you need you will receive.
So hope, and every day
believe it will come true so much
that it has no other option than to give it to you."

my vow

Today I accept the things I cannot change.
I trust that everything in my life is perfectly aligned.
I let go of the urge to control and allow the Universe
to take the reins knowing that all my needs are being
wonderfully met at all times.

silence

Can you hear it?
The whispers from your soul.
It's your Higher Self calling you.
Shh.
Just be still.
Be present.
Close your eyes
and take a deep breath.
Listen—
You are being told the way forward.
Can you hear it?

surrender

With every breath, I become more myself.
More me, more in touch with the Divine within.
I inhale confidence and wisdom
as I open the channel to my intuition.
And as I exhale I release anything
that holds me back from being true to me.
All the limiting beliefs, the grief,
the lies I tell myself.
I let go of all the things
causing me unhappiness and pain.
With each breath,
I gift myself peace and harmony.
Surrendering wholeheartedly into myself,
to love, and closer towards my dreams.

belief

This belief of being alone
and disconnected from the world
is all your own creation.
And if you search for truth
to support that idea
you will be sure to find it.
But what if…
You changed your belief into connectedness?
Into togetherness?
Into we are one?
And find the proof that shows you are loved
and supported by the Divine always?
Imagine what kind of life you could lead knowing
that everything around you is your creation,
and that your creation is beautiful and magical,
and incredibly unique to what it is that you need to
achieve in this lifetime.

sunburnt

Sometimes I feel like I give too much love.
My heart beats like the sun,
an endless beam of light,
shooting love in all directions.
Warming the Earth and burning everything it
touches.

discipline

I'm still trying to figure out my own power.
Still trying to learn what it means
to stand entirely on my own.
At times I am fragile and tender as a flower
waiting for the next man to pick me up and carry me
in his pocket.
But that shouldn't be the way to live.
For I have roots that connect
to the abundance of life below.
I can water myself and grow
as miraculous as I wish.
If I am another's prize,
I limit myself to confinement.
Choosing to sit on a table in a vase for their show.
When in truth,
I need to endure all the seasons,
drown in the rainfall,
and burn beneath the sun.
Feel the loving support from every element
of the Earth's vibrations,
every emotion,
every starvation.
So that I may rise into a magnificent creation,
a profound existence,
the beautiful movement of energy
that I was destined to become.

strength

If I don't face it this lifetime,
if I don't allow myself to heal…
It will come back again and again
in the next lifetime and the next one after that.
And it will pour into the hearts
of the children who come after me.
I have the power here and now
to heal myself and stop the pain
from continuing for thousands of generations.
It's going to get uncomfortable
but I have to keep going.

let it be

Don't be afraid to fall, to break.
It's a chance to rebuild yourself,
an opportunity for rebirth.
Enter into that darkness
and transform it into the light.
So that the person you become
stands much stronger than before.
And next time,
you won't fall down
so willingly
again.

heal

Send love to those who have done you wrong.
It's through forgiveness that we heal.

—

to keep

In order to heal, we need to forgive.
So, that's what I'm doing.
Today I take back my power.
Today I forgive and release you.
I know now that we were all just trying to survive,
all just trying to live the best we knew how.
No one is to blame.
No one "won."
We all lost, but we all learned a life lesson
and that, my friend,
is one of the most valuable things we can own.
No one can take that away from us now.

discover

Inside every choice, I was shown the truth.
Through every pain, healing was found.
With every mistake, another layer of
where I did not love myself was revealed,
and so for that, I am thankful.

telescope

What do you carry in your heart?
If you hold love,
you will see love everywhere you look.
If you hold sadness,
the whole world around you will mirror that pain.
So let go all the broken promises,
the shattered dreams,
and deep wounds within your mind.
Be free of your heartache,
your pain, and your stress.
Allow beautiful, loving light energy to move through
into this space.
Then you will see the world in all its glory —
an incredible and magical place to be.

fulfilment

When she was hungry, the Earth fed her.
When she was thirsty, the waters quenched her.
When she felt cold, the sun warmed her
And when she couldn't breathe,
the Universe whispered sweet love songs
into her lungs, bringing forth the beauty
that was lying dormant in her Soul.

forgiveness

Forgive yourself for every time you put their feelings
first instead of your own.
For every time you said yes
when you really meant no.
For every time you thought they wouldn't hurt you
and they did.
Forgive yourself.
You have carried this weight around for long enough,
you did the best that you knew
how to at the time.
Now is the time to let it go.

limits

I forgive you, and I send love to you.
Even if you cut me down with actions of anger,
words of hate, or thoughts of sadness.
Desperately trying to link me back to the dark
shadows, where you rest so peacefully troubled.
Yes, I will still be sending love to you.
This is my gift of unconditional love to you.
There are no limits, I hold no judgment,
only endless compassion.
You can never hurt me,
because you see,
that would mean that I'm hurting myself,
and I've come too far to ever do that again.

confidence

She plays with the real world
just long enough to appear normal.
But when nighttime falls she becomes truly alive.
Beneath the moon and the stars she wanders.
Dancing with the vibrations of the Universe,
she opens her heart.
Gathering inspiration, wisdom, and beauty.
If only she had the courage to show the world
what she found.

revelation

I see what you're hiding—
a beautiful Soul inside a magnificent body.
Yet, why aren't you showing
the world the Real You?
Why are you concealing your talents?
Dumbing yourself down to "fit in".
There is magic, and rainbows,
and miracles being swallowed.
Just because you are too scared
of what will happen if you do.
I'll tell you what will happen —
You will live happily ever after.
The end.

letters to myself, part 3

Enough is enough.
It's time to step up and fulfill
what it is that you are destined to do.
And you can't do it with all this negative self-talk
or with an insecure attitude.
You are a glistening delight
of innovative energy,
overflowing with endless talent
and creative dreams.
Success is coming to you,
in every way possible,
and it's going to be more spectacular
than you could ever imagine.
That day is coming soon.
Don't give up now.

magic potion

There is beauty within you.
It's a never-ending vessel
full of love, dignity and care.
It's available to you always.
But sometimes it might feel empty
and maybe today is one of those days.
And that's okay.
You just need to refuel.
Get out into nature
and feel the ground beneath your toes.
The sun on your face, water on your skin,
and fresh air on your breath.
Take a moment to remember how brilliant you are.
How strong your mind is.
How incredibly talented you can be
if you just set your mind to all that is within you.
Breathe in and out deeply
as you pour a glass of love
from the vessel in your heart.
But this time, label it for yourself
and drink it all up.

smoke

There is a fire within you,
burning brightly,
growing stronger.
Every time you feel weak,
that fire is still there.
Waiting to be acknowledged.
It's blazing with or without your consent.
It will never diminish,
it will only blaze wilder.
It's up to you to let that light shine through you,
and it's all within your power to spread warmth
to those who pass you by.
It's your duty to allow the flame to light up your life,
and it would be a tragedy to die without ever
letting the fire breathe.

awake

I look to you for definition
and yet it is me upon whom I should call.
For the words you say are lost on deaf ears,
absorbed in my own insecurity,
and your praises disperse
as hurriedly as the clouds in the night sky.
But if I were to reveal the truth
and open my heart to see
that the Divine sleeps within you
the same as she sleeps within me.

liberty

Give yourself permission
to breathe,
to live,
to laugh,
to love.
For the Divine Spirit sleeps within you,
ready to be awoken.
Ready to be set free.
Ready to vibrate the colors of the rainbow
in between the tiny spaces of non-existence.

Give yourself permission to say no.
To spend time on your own.
To set boundaries and follow through with them.
To leave bad relationships.
To change careers, houses, cities, countries.
You are allowed to grow into a better version of you.
A better kind of you.
You staying small isn't helping anyone,
it is only destroying yourself.

intuitive fate

When you listen to the
passionate cravings of your Soul,
the Universe is listening too,
and the path of your destiny is woven,
carefully laid out,
waiting for you.

conversations with the moon

She felt different after we talked.
She said she just thought of her life as her mind
and her body and that was it.
There was no soul.
No inner voice guiding her.
No worshiping of the sun, the Earth,
the sea, or the air.
She never thought it was okay to love herself.
To praise the Godly Creator within her own heart.
But when she finally let go
of the control in her mind,
and allowed the Universe to take over,
that's when the real magic happened.
That's when she discovered
that there was Infinite Wisdom surrounding her.
Delivering her all the right messages
at exactly the perfect time.
She just needed to close her eyes to see it
for what it was.

harmony

When she walked through the door she felt different somehow. She understood her body and her mind and that sometimes life doesn't go to plan and that's okay, that sometimes she needs to just let go of ideas or concepts or expectations and just see the world that day for what it is. Knowing that whatever she was going through was preparing her for the person she needed to become. Knowing that the world at this moment on this day was beautiful and that she too mirrored that perfection.

mermaid wishes

The blood moon rose in the horizon.
I sat on the rocks, on the beach as I listened to the
sounds of the water kissing the sand.
And together with me they prayed.
I whispered my wishes and dreams into the wind,
and I watched as the seas carried them to the moon.
The stars twinkled as though they were listening.
It was a wink from the Universe telling me that the
right dreams will come true.

la luna

I am breathing deeply as I inhale her strength.
There is nothing but love surrounding me.
An abundance of light dances at my feet,
and it bounces up through to my heart.
Spreading forth from the inside of my hands.
And I echo her vibrations.
Moving my body in harmonic bliss.
Declaring my love for her, she shines brighter.
And together we give and receive our love.
Creating and defining a perfect world
that we wish to share.
I ignite my destiny and steer my fate
as I whisper my prayers in her ear.
This year, this month, this day,
I wish for everything that has been manifested to
come into fruition.

revive

This is your rebirth.
Your past has healed,
your Soul has evolved to a new level.
These last few months have been challenging
but it was necessary to rebirth
into a new you.
An improved you in every level.
Mentally, spiritually, and physically.
You asked for change, well here it is.
It's yours to keep.

commit

I have awoken with a desire to be a better me.
To love more, to give more, to help more.
To listen more to myself and those around me.
To be honest with myself and the actions of others.
And above and foremost,
I make a vow today to honor my boundaries.
Bless me with the courage to walk away from
anything that does not raise my vibration higher.
And in doing so, I will forever remember that I am
guided by the Universe on every step of my journey.

matured

Today, I am no longer spending my time
on childish reactions.
I can control my voice, my hands and my thoughts.
I do not have to speak negatively.
I choose to speak with love and be still with love.
And open my heart to see the truth.
For this unhealthy behavior is no longer serving me.
So, today I make a change.
Today I step forward and never look back.
Today I choose life,
I choose Love, and peace and happiness.
Today I have awoken a healthy routine within,
to ground myself in my body.
I gift myself time to be with me,
to honor and respect who I am
and where I am going.
By giving gratitude I will attract Eternal Bliss.
Today, I forgive myself for my unhealthy attitude.
Perfection is merely a perception.
I am excited about life.
I'm re-energized and ready for the day ahead.
I am learning new things about myself.
What I like and don't like.
And it's okay, it's a positive change.
It's the recipe for self-improvement.

unconscious

I close my eyes and journey deep within.
Diving wholeheartedly into
a blank landscape of nothingness.
Yet despite its vast empire
of "the unknown"
it's the safest I've ever felt.
And the more me I've ever been.
In this space, I breathe with great relief..
For every breath brings me closer to myself,
closer to the Divine Light within my being,
the Soul inside this body.
And the more that I connect
with that version of myself,
The better I feel, the clearer I can see,
and the more supported I feel by the Universe.

eternal spirit

I am always with you,
yet you cannot see me.
You can never touch me,
but I know you can feel me.
I hide within your heart and yet I am everywhere.
I am the only one who will walk your path,
the only one who will ever know you
your greatest failures and highest triumphs,
I will be there,
whispering love notes into your mind.
I will never leave you.
You are never alone.

i am listening

In my sacred space,
I open my heart and listen
to what my Soul truly desires.
She tells me to be brave, passionate, wild and free.
And I am willing to follow through
with whatever Source tells me.
For She is the creator of my life and will always want
the very best for me.

She tells me to ground my Soul in my body.
So that I may claim my space here on Earth.
For when I do, I will understand
the true depth of my existence,
And I will see my life with clarity
as I go about my day.
My life is blessed with love and respect
if I so choose it, and with ease,
I open my mind to change.
For I am resilient, graceful, and confident.
And I am the creator of my world, here to stay.

unlimited

She wakes up scared.
Not of what she can't do, but of what she can.
She has the power to create whatever she wants.
The ability to be whoever she wishes to be.
But all that power somehow suffocates her.
And she falls down worried with guilt
as to what other people might think
if she ever showed them her power.
Scared that if she steps out of the crowd that she's
going to stand out too much.
But she has no choice.
She has to follow her dreams.
If she doesn't they will haunt her all day.
Remind her of the kind of girl she is meant to be.
The kind of girl she deep down wants to be.
And one day she listens.
She is no longer lost.
She is finally free.

be still

I am ready for a change but I feel stuck in my feet.
Unsure where to move to.
And so I breathe.
I close my eyes
and feel the strength of my Soul within.
Listen to my heart to what it is that I truly need.
And I focus on that.
I trust the timing of my life and flow with gratitude
in accordance to my surroundings.
Not everything needs to move all of a sudden.
Not everything has to change all of the time.
Sometimes we have more signs to be revealed,
more truths to uncover.
There are lessons to be seen even if we feel
as though we are bored.
Boredom is a lesson in itself.

leap

She is conflicted internally
between who she is and who she wants to be.
Unable to shake the feeling of regret
and past mistakes
to step into her divine self, completely.
There is something holding her back.
But if only she were to throw away
all those limiting beliefs,
all those negative thoughts that did her no good.
And realize that they did not define her.
That she created her own definition, her own
vocabulary for who she was,
who she is and where she is going.

clarity

I finally know why I have such regret --
because I am denying the voice of my own intuition.

conserve

Sometimes I like to escape from my real life.
And enter a quiet moment where I can be surrounded
in solitude. I disappear amongst the rubble of white
noise and street traffic. Sometimes in dusty corners of
the beat-up café in the middle of nowhere, where no
one is watching. I hide there. Staring from afar at the
beautiful weirdness of life around me. Attempting to
make sense of this peculiar readiness.
Unearthed. Unjust and unfair.
Yet somehow, it is perfect.

to see the world

It's just another crowd.
Different colored lights in a new hot spot city.
It changes colors as often as it changes faces
and the time passes through slower than expected.
But we still push through.
And the food still tastes good.
Although our connections with people
are sometimes jaded,
we still give them a chance.
The strange sounds that come without warning.
It's the sounds of life moving,
it pours through uncontrollably.
Like the rain,
washing the lush greenery in the forest.
Where the frogs and the butterflies and the leeches
breathe, sometimes I talk to them.
They tell me about the lands that I am yet to see.
They whisper the truth of my own people.
One day we will unite together, and share the
wisdom of our ancestors.

palm

We carry the weight of the world in our hands.
We have the power for change,
for life,
for death.
And yet why do we believe that we are weak?
That we are incapable of love?
That we can't go on, sometimes?
It's because we forget.
That we created the world with our hands.
That we steer our destiny with our hands.
We create a life around us,
and we destroy it just as easily.
All with the simplicity of just our hands.

addiction

The moon is plump and full of energy.
The love of shining brightly, it's her time.
Like a silent musical she lies still
and we are addicted to her blushing.
The clouds shy her away.
But they act as we merely wish — to be closer to her.

nurture

I lie with my chest to the ground, and
it is as though the Earth has an anchor in my heart.
And it's connecting me closer to you.
I don't want to move.
Too enamored with the nurture of your love.
Utterly obsessed with the vibrations in my heart,
from just your breath of life.
And as I close my eyes and open my heart to receive
your blessings,
I mold into myself.
Letting my Soul completely rejuvenate,
and refresh,
and thrive,
as it has always meant to do.

to be free

It was as though she had opened her eyes
for the very first time.
She could feel her guides by her side.
Her body and soul reunited
and her senses rehabilitated.
She was on top of the world.
Soaring high through the stars she flew
in between the dark spaces of
black matter.
She shone brightly.
A blazing flame of stardust
that danced through the air
and breathed in the light.

today

I stand with confidence in my skin,
as I claim my space here on Earth.
I walk with pride and speak with passion.
I am living the life I want to.
Because it is the life I am choosing to.
My inner peace is strong,
My creativity ignited.
My Soul speaks words of encouragement.
Telling me I am on the right path,
whispering love songs through my heart.
I am falling in love with life
all over again with every new day,
in every breath,
as I walk in alignment with my Higher Self.

gentle

For the first time in a long time,
I feel in harmony with the vibrations of the Universe.
My heart is beating to the sound of the gentle
glistening light that is my Soul inside my Being.
And from the centre of my heart,
my life flows organically in peace around me.
As the Universe dances hand in hand with the Divine
Spirit who resides within my body.

her

She loves herself unconditionally.
There is no judgment, no pressure to be
anyone else other than who she is.
And with gratitude, she flourishes.

She graces the world with the most beautiful
feminine energy ever seen, heard, or felt.
Her power of self-respect encourages everyone
around her to do the same.
And her life is filled with authenticity,
heart-warming conversations,
deep soul connections,
and joyous celebrations for all.

She is walking her truth.
Each step more brave, bolder than the last.
She is unapologetically raw, beautiful, and carefree.
And as a result,
her life overflows with love around her,
in rhythmic purrs,
in perfect alignment with the beating of her heart.

infinite

She floats between the worlds of the seen and unseen.
Gathering ancient wisdom and angelic energy
wherever she goes.
She plays with fire
and yet is the one who ignites the flame.
For she knows that everything is her creation,
both her failures and her successes.
And so she moves with courage on her journey,
entering the darkness with fierce strength.
Every time she falls, she stands up smiling.
Laughing at the irony of herself pushing her down.
Her essence reflects a dance
between the mystical and wonderful,
an intoxicating love potion to devour in a world that
overflows with forgotten beauty and magic.
For she knows that experience
is what her purpose here on Earth is,
and with full force she explores all that there is, all
that there could be, and all that there was.
She knows what she must endure,
she knows it's the only way forward.
And yet sometimes she doubts herself,
as to whether she can go on.
"You have created this for yourself."
She laughs.
It's time to unlearn, relearn, and grow.

angel

It is a divine feeling to be as One with the Universe. To completely surrender yourself wholeheartedly, and allow the Universe to not only catch you but raise you so high that you fly with the wings that you've always had but had forgotten about.

rainbows

She fulfills her cravings with nature's blessings.
And her Soul sings soundly in a peaceful bliss.
Her essence derives from internal beauty,
and her love overflows the way the stardust falls,
creating magic wherever it goes.

lullaby

She honors the Divine within.
Giving back to herself through self-nurturing care.
And her inner-child has healed,
as the voice of her spirit speaks louder.
Every day she becomes more and more herself.
And her Soul thanks her for it,
dancing with grace, harmoniously through life.

decisions

When you choose to live in alignment
with Your Divine Self
a love will radiate from the core of your essence,
creating a dance of beauty upon your skin.
It will magnetize all who witness your enchantment
as you gift them with your elegance and the blessings
from the Universe.

home

It's taken me a while, but I finally feel myself again.
Better than I've been before.
The water has cleansed and revitalized me.
Gifting me the clarity and fluidity
of my words and movements.
And I feel at ease,
as I float between the rivers of time.
Blessed and divine,
grateful and nourished.

risk

It's time to open your heart to love.
It's time to forgive those who've hurt you.
Because this pain won't go away on its own,
and this blame won't shift until you move it.
It's time to let go.
It's time to open your heart to love again.

imprint

I enter today with an open heart.
I'm overflowing with love to share
with those who pass me by.
And I choose to let go of the past,
I have healed from it, felt the pain,
and I know the reasons why.
It was because I needed to see the world differently.
I had to be shaken and realigned
with the person I needed to become.
There's no turning back now.
I am here to stay, and so
I mark my day with love.

locket

When you see him you will know,
for no one else will have ever felt so real.
When you meet him you will understand why every
other relationship couldn't work out,
and you'll be so relieved that you didn't settle.
He's on his way, he's coming.
He's everything you've ever wanted and more.
He will never let you doubt yourself
or his loyalty to you,
for he is you,
and you are he,
and there is no breaking a love
that was built from lifetimes before.

stained memories

My love.
It took a while to find you but here you are,
standing before me as if time has never passed.
I touch your skin and I remember
your smell from lifetimes ago.
I've never felt more at peace
or more at home
than when I am by your side.
You are everything I've ever wanted and more.
I feel secure in myself and in my love for you.
I have trust in you and us.
I know you will never hurt me,
I know you will always do what's best for us.
I know we are together forever,
in this life and the next.

feeding

Amidst your energy, I feel alive.
And like a vampire, I feed my hunger.
Your taste gives life back into my Soul.
But this greed is not in vain,
for I give back all that I have taken.
An equal exchange of power to play,
a constant cycle
of loving vibrations…
We pick each other up
and twist each other around.
An energy frenzy of play and sleep.
A reunion
between two long-lost lovers from lifetimes before.
A rare connection of intimacy
that cannot be explained
and need never be explained for
it just is
and always has been.

support

My heart blazes in flames,
growing from the comfort of your breath.
I feel your love within me.
My love is your love.
Our souls entwined, it's like we are the same.
Two pieces broken apart now together,
there is no undoing us now, we are molded as one.
I have never felt more myself until I met you.
More me, more real, more true.
You give me the confidence to be the best me
I know how to.
And I feel stronger with you by my side.
I'm not scared about anything
for I know you will help me through it.
My love.
Our souls forever entwined from this day forward.
My heart blazes across a million stars,
burning brightly in the comfort of your presence.
We are fulfilling the promises engraved inside our
heart.

emotions

I wish to take pieces of the world
and put them together into one.
I would start with your smile.
And that shimmer in your eye
when you look at me.
The way you laugh
when I tickle your skin.
The sound of your voice
when you say my name.
And as I put together my list
I realize, my ideal world
is not a place,
but a feeling,
of what it's like to be loved by you.

heaven

Tonight you fell asleep in my arms.
And I smelled your skin while feeling your heartbeat
and listening to the soft purring rhythm of your
breath.

You are so beautiful.

We talked for hours about the life we want to build
together, and you confided in me your goals for the
future and how I would be intricately woven
throughout them.

Everything you say and do
makes my love grow deeper.
There is no one else.
It is you and only you.

My love, mon amour,
thank you for coming into my life.

secrets of the universe

And together we sit in silence.
Staring in awe at the painted masterpiece
that dances amongst the night sky.
The stars glisten in words,
speaking a language of truth
too difficult to comprehend,
a conversation of infinite intelligence
that is unable to be defined.
But together we will try.
We'll talk about all the things we love,
our future, family, and home.
And together we will write our dreams in the stars,
but the words are already there,
our destiny is waiting for us to take them.
There is nothing left to do but breathe and smile
and feel the answers within ourselves.
Enjoy the serenity.
This profound moment of existence
that only a few can truly see.

fear

I stay quiet.
While an explosion of thoughts echo in my mind.
And I struggle to find the right words to say.
And when I do find them, I'm terrified of what you
might think. Terrified of what you might do.
Will you think I'm crazy? Will you think I'm weak?
And so I pretend.
I hide behind a bright smile and curious eyes.
Forever shifting the forms from what's here to what's
really there. Waiting for the trust to be built.
So strong. So strong.
That nothing I can say or do will shake it and you
will never break it.
Hold me safely in your arms, my darling.
I cannot see the night alone.
I cannot hold the space without you.
The light is too bright.
I find comfort in the shadows
but you are nowhere there.
Good. Because we'd be a pair of miserable ones
had you suffered too.
Instead, you see the beauty in everything.
Like a child, pure and innocent and endearing.
You. Beautiful. Loving. You.
A pure, blissful heart of grace. Of good grace.
Here to remind me that there is light in me too.

soul mates

There is a love engraved in the root of my heart.
It is a promise we made from lifetimes before.
A commitment that lives for eternity.
A vow that bypasses the logic of time and space,
and connects us together for infinity and beyond.
Our love is never-ending.
Our love is all that matters.
Finding you in this life will be easy,
because we made a promise to each other from
lifetimes before.

to my love

I lie with you
skin to skin,
my body absorbed in your comfort.
And I feel as though my heart stops beating.
I feel at ease.
Past my body, I move.
And my Soul rejoices with yours.
As the energy of our love combines
into one great big beating heart.
And the beat of our song echoes through our lives
in a sweet melody.
Strumming with courage, commitment, and support.
And our song continues to evolve
through the fabric of time.
Growing louder and stronger as the days go by.
The drumming of our hearts began many lives
before, and our song will continue to beat for an
eternity more.

encircled

I counted the freckles on his chest
as he lay there beside me.
Each circle marked an entire universe on its own.
it was the depth upon which I loved him.

enamored

There are no words beautiful enough
to describe the way I feel about you.
It's a feeling that takes over my entire body
and overflows from within my heart.
And my heart beats uncontrollably with too much
strength from how much I love you.
And sometimes I can't breathe because
I love you so much.
There is only one thing that calms me and that is
when I hold you and feel your heart touching mine.

this is us

You and me.
Open-hearted and bursting smiles.
Willing to love and risk everything at once.
Look into my eyes and feel your way to the truth.
There is a love shining brightly
inside of me just for you.
This flame has been alight
since the beginning of time.
An explosion of stardust that encircles around my
heart and it bursts in euphoric bliss
as we love each other day by day.
And the flame lives with peace,
knowing our commitment to making it work.

Any challenges we face only make us stronger.
For we know that hidden in every fight is a wounded
inner child, combating the fear of rejection, the fear of
not being good enough, the fear of true love.

But if you dare show me your vulnerability,
I will hold space to heal this together.
With nurturing words, and gentle patience.
We will move through our lives side by side.
Because our heart and soul are entwined together,
beating as one.
This is us.

gratitude

Everything about you is divine.
The way you love, the way you spread kindness
despite the struggles you face.
The way you inspire me
to be a better version of myself.
Everything about you I adore
and I am so thankful that you are in my life.

completion

Through the warmth of your eyes,
the light inside of me is ignited.
And when I hear your voice
I feel the beauty within me
that I thought had disappeared.
As I touch your skin
you bring my attention to the present moment.
And when I tell you that I love you,
I know that I am welcoming happiness into my life,
as I fulfill my destiny with you by my side.

waking

I am lying in bed next to you, watching you sleep.
Feeling the warmth of your body and your soft
breath
and heartbeat.
And it is still not enough.
I need more.
I can't wait to spend all day by your side.
Together we play through life, dancing and singing
praises of our own love story.
And I cherish every second together until you go
back to sleep and I lie here once more
watching you dream,
waiting for you to wake up.

facts

Meeting your soul mate doesn't complete you,
because you, yourself, are already complete.
But the union of two souls coming together will bring
your vibration into a whole new level.
For when your love connects it will ignite a fire in
your heart that you have never felt before. That fire
will burst through your essence and illuminate your
life in a way you have never seen before. And that
love that lights your day will shower onto everyone
around you, magnifying and intensifying your
journey here on Earth.

you

There's nothing that you do that goes unnoticed.
That kind smile to a stranger,
that love that overflows
in abundance from your heart
when you listen to me.
The infinite times that you help me, care for me,
feed me, clean for me.
Every action, every movement of your worth,
we all see how beautiful you are.
You are pouring love from the center of your Soul,
from the core of your being.
And we are all doing exactly this:
falling more and more in love with you.

idealism

But what if…
we all consumed ourselves entirely in love,
just by thinking love and exuding love.
Maybe, the power of us together would ignite a fire
so strong, so fierce, that it would flare throughout the
whole world, and our Earth will become what it was
once before— a flaming ball of stardust circling the
endless sky.

the blessing

This year, this month, this day, this moment.
I bring my manifestations into fruition.
I invite health, wealth, and blessings
to myself and my loved ones.
May we all live in alignment with our Divine Truth.
May we together walk confidently toward the
directions of our dreams.
And bring forth clarity as we fulfill our life purpose.
Let us walk hand in hand on this journey we call life,
and share our love with each other
so that we may heal the world.

here now

I am flowing with the Universe.
Dancing amongst my dreams,
creating and inspiring the world around me.
I am stronger than yesterday, wiser than before.
And now I walk boldly with confidence,
spreading love and peace
from the centre of my being.

whisper

Every night I talk to the stars and the moon.
I tell them all the things that I love in my life
and they whisper the secrets of the Universe to me.

unity

She walks without fear,
spreading acts of love and light
wherever she goes.
A healing touch here,
a gentle word there.
She is an angel,
a blessing to this world.
"This is God's will," she says
when asked of why such kindness.

"No one should ever feel alone." she says
as she covers you with loving kisses.
She holds your hand
and with smiling eyes she says,
"I am only a reflection of
the love you hold in your heart."

the future

I have dreamed of you since I was a child.
And from that day forth I have been obsessed with
becoming every bit the same as you.
It the best version of myself, the person I wish to be.
It is a desire to bring forth my gifts to the world.
And this hunger for success continues to grow,
as the steps to my dream lay out before me.

This thought is an evolving dimension,
a combination of energy, space, and time.
And it is up to me to lay the pieces of the puzzle,
to take what it is, that is already mine.
So rise up my friend as you journey with me.
We will together walk this path as one,
For the love never flows unless you are near me.
And it is you, my Higher Self, who I wish to become.

newness

In all my life I have never felt so calm as I do now.
The most grounded, the most in my skin.
Such a surreal feeling of knowing
that I am on the right path.
No more confusion, sadness or despair.
Only love, happiness, and excitement awaits.

I have let go of fear,
of the assumption of inadequacy.
And left all feelings of negativity behind.
I know I am worthy of love, of wisdom and miracles
and they will enter my life in abundance
for I am a magnet attracting profound beauty
and all that there is to come.

the truth

Her smile was contagious.
It felt like magic the way
it blossomed from within her Soul,
Rubbing off onto everyone who passed her by.
Strangers, friends, they all looked at her and
wondered, how she had come to be so happy.
But the truth was; she hid behind that smile,
Nursing a heartbreak and a disappointed childhood.
And that unsettling feeling of not being complete.
The questions in her mind never went away.
Who was she and why was she here?
All she could do was smile.
It was her only weapon
to create the change she desired.
And it was her only medicine
to heal all the grief that she felt.
For when she smiled
the world didn't seem so grim anymore.
And she didn't feel so alone anymore.
She had figured out a new way to love herself,
And it was working.

oak

Within me is an eternal bliss,
A river of hope.
A voice of reason
that washes love over every problem.
And that peace you wish to seek,
I hold it within.
It shines so brightly in my world
that your words cannot shake me,
nor your actions cannot break me.
The only way for the destruction
is by the hand of my own.
But my body is rooted in the ground,
and I am supported by more than you know.
I am too strong within my own mind,
too wise from the grace of the Universe.
And there is too much love in my heart.
So try as you may,
but beware,
this love of mine is contagious.

the conductor

I am grateful for my past
for it's shaped me who I am today.
And it's provoked a spiritual awakening
within my being;
the realization that we are more
than just our body and mind.
We are souls,
dancing together in the mystical realms of
enchantment,
moving elegantly and gracefully
to the Universe's beating heart,
amongst a song playing that we call "life."

spiritual awakening

I finally feel like I am living
the life that I was meant to.
Surrounded by nature and enamored
in the presence of her beauty,
I breathe with gratitude.
Inhaling fresh air to lighten my mind,
as I cleanse my body with the salt water seas,
and kiss my skin with sunshine.
Admiring the miraculous day
gifted from the Universe.
And as nighttime falls I, too, glisten like the stars.
Shining my Soul,
I absorb the vibrations of the moon.
And as I sleep,
I rest my head on a pillow of sweet perfume,
healing my body as I dream.
I finally understand that everything is from within.
And I thank you, I love you
for choosing this body,
for living the life I want to live.
Knowing that every choice is mine.

elegance

I do everything with Grace,
with gratitude and honor,
I watch the transformation of my body.
The strength it has gained,
the color of my skin as it soaks up
the delicious kisses from the sun.
And I put moisture back into my skin,
rejuvenating and reviving.
Carefully stroking each leg, my tummy, and back.

I am creating a body I am proud of.
And I nurture it
with the blessings from the Universe.
There is no one else to take control of it,
it is my haven, my sanctuary.
Thank you for choosing me.
Thank you for choosing this body, dear Soul.

she

She is the creator,
She carries forth the wisdom of our ancestors.
She is powerful and magnificent,
graceful and kind.
She is the Divine Goddess
and she walks among us.

listen

You are perfect
exactly the way you are.
You are beautiful and talented and no one can ever
take that away from you.
You are worthy of miracles to bless your life.
You are loved, irreplaceable.
You are enough.

replenished

Now I can breathe easy.
Refreshed, revitalized, and nourished.
Cleansed with clarity.
The sun, the sand, the water,
nature, Earth.
It's all I need in life.
You can find me barefoot,
under the sun,
eating with my hands,
singing with my heart,
dancing with the clouds,
following my truth.

destiny

She appeared to know herself
and it showed so beautifully.
I believed in her.
Whatever she decided to do with her life,
I knew it would happen.
Because she wrote her dreams
with the glimmer of the star-kissed sky
and prayed with love upon every full moon.
When the sun appeared, she sang her blessings
sweetly, with more praises, more glory,
more higher wisdom revealed.
Those who knew her shared stories of her travels, for
she exceeded all expectations,
defied all limiting beliefs,
as she opened herself up to a world that she had
created.

authenticity

She is beautiful,
not just because she is pretty,
but because she lives
in alignment with her
Divine Truth.

orderly

God has a plan for you.
So you have to stop doubting it.
And you have to keep going.
Keep smiling,
keep living from that place of love within you.
Because very soon things are going to get easier,
and everything will make sense.
And you will laugh and be so very grateful
that you didn't give up.

bliss

When you choose to live from your Heart Center
where Universal Source resides.
The vibrations from your Soul beat loudly
And your level of consciousness expands out,
blessing your life and everyone around you in
harmonic bliss.

sparkle

You are a shimmer of loving light
that vibrates for an eternity.
You are destined to create incredible things,
don't ever forget it.

here

Stand tall, stand proud.
You are One.
You are God.
You are everything
you want to be and more.
Do not listen to the noise.
You are safe.
You are loved.

forever

I breathe with ease knowing that
the Universe is looking after me.
I spread love unconditionally
for I feel all the blessings surrounding me.
I don't worry about what comes my way
because I know my Soul is guiding me.
Everything in my life is my creation,
giving depth and meaning to my day.

eternity

The journey to reveal my true self
continues to evolve
as I slowly strip to reveal
the forgotten pieces of me.

about the author

Phoebe Garnsworthy

Phoebe Garnsworthy is an Australian female author who seeks to discover magic in everyday life. She has travelled the world extensively, exploring eastern and western philosophies alike, while studying the influences that these beliefs have on humanity.

The intention of her writing is to encourage conscious living and unconditional love.

www.PhoebeGarnsworthy.com

Made in the USA
San Bernardino, CA
23 March 2020

65950391R00109